Cartoon Characters Coloring Books For Kids

Coloring Pages for Kids

By Gala Publication

PUBLISHED BY:

Gala Publication

ISBN-13: 978- 1508815877
ISBN-10: 1508815879

©Copyright 2015 – Gala Publication

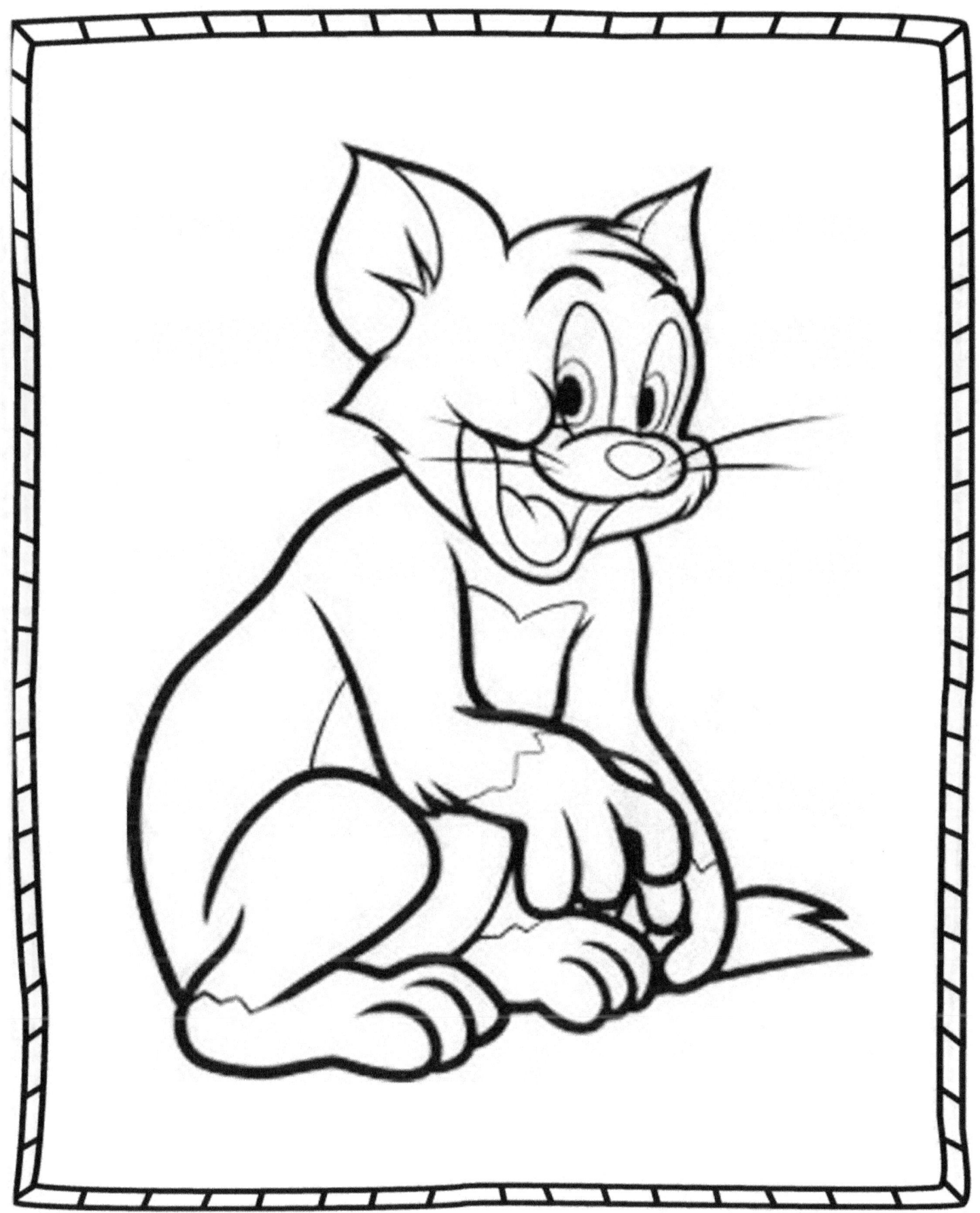

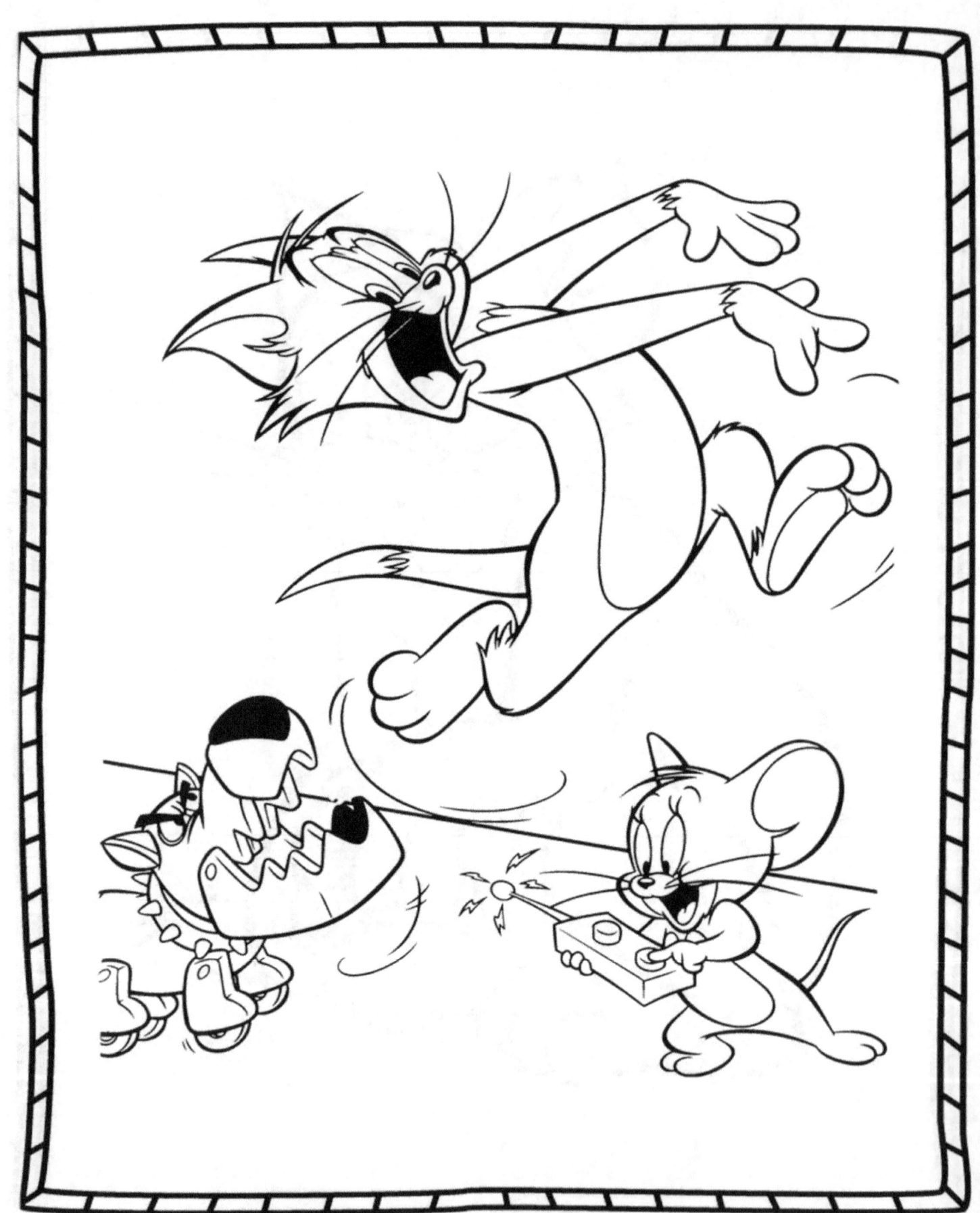

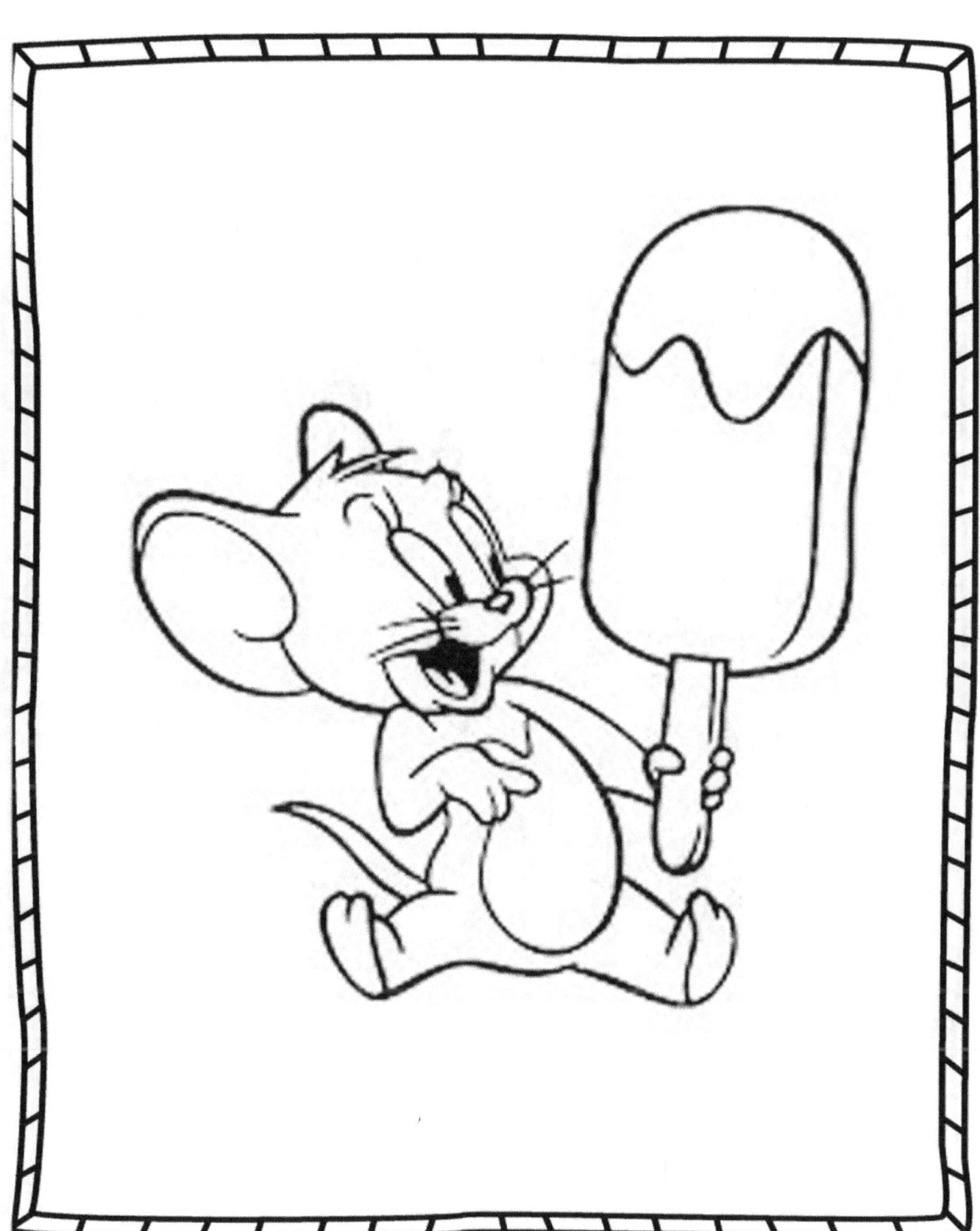

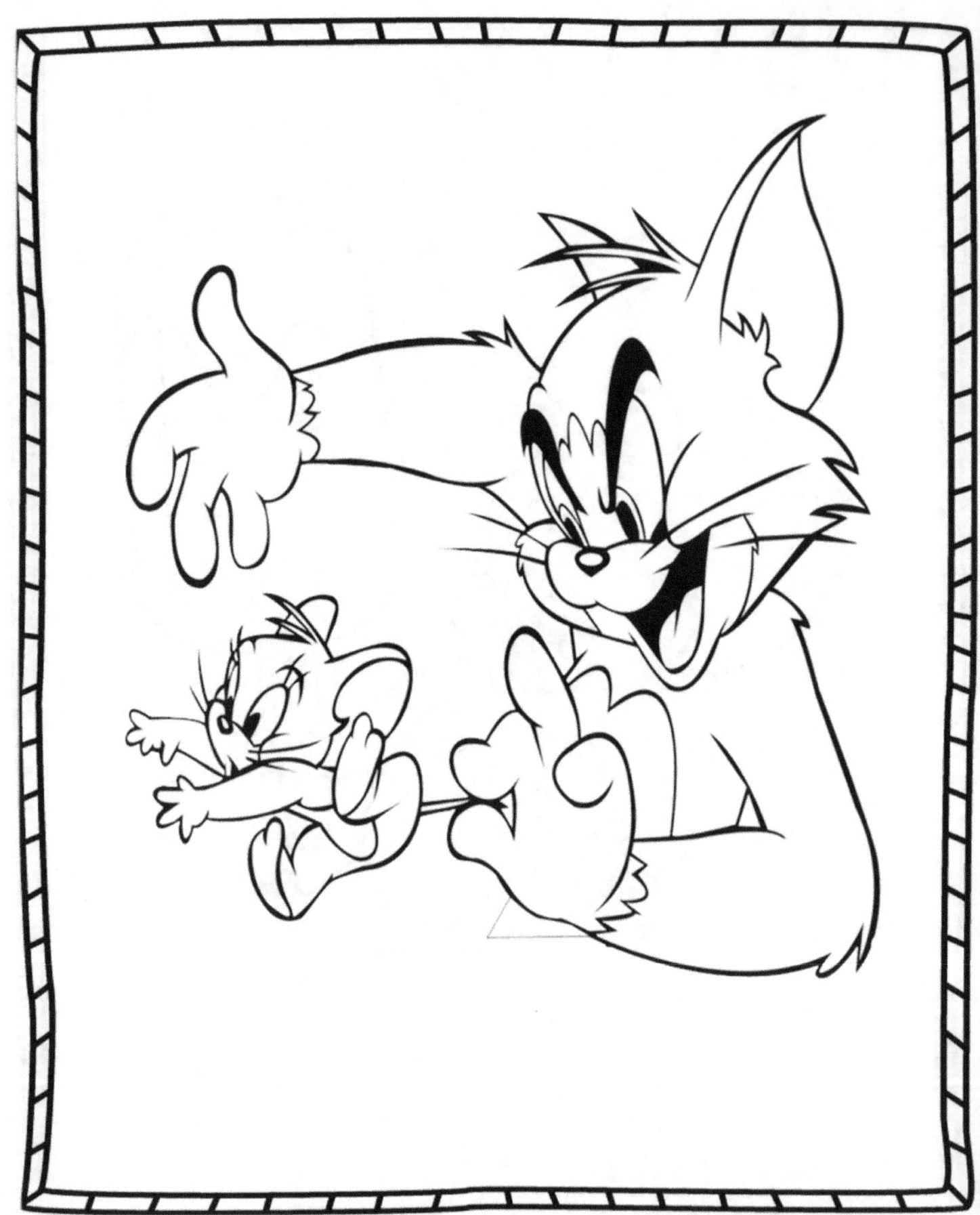

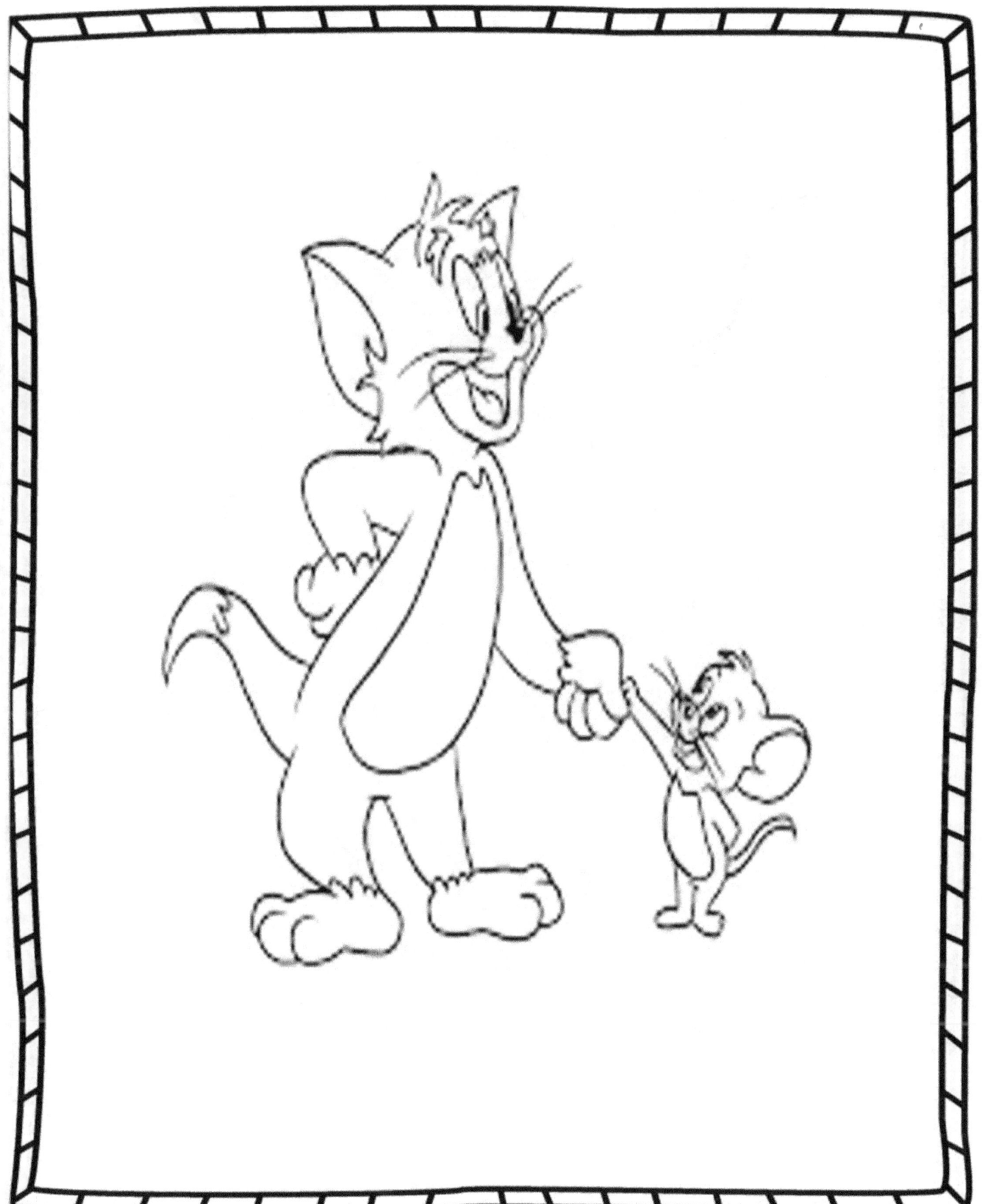

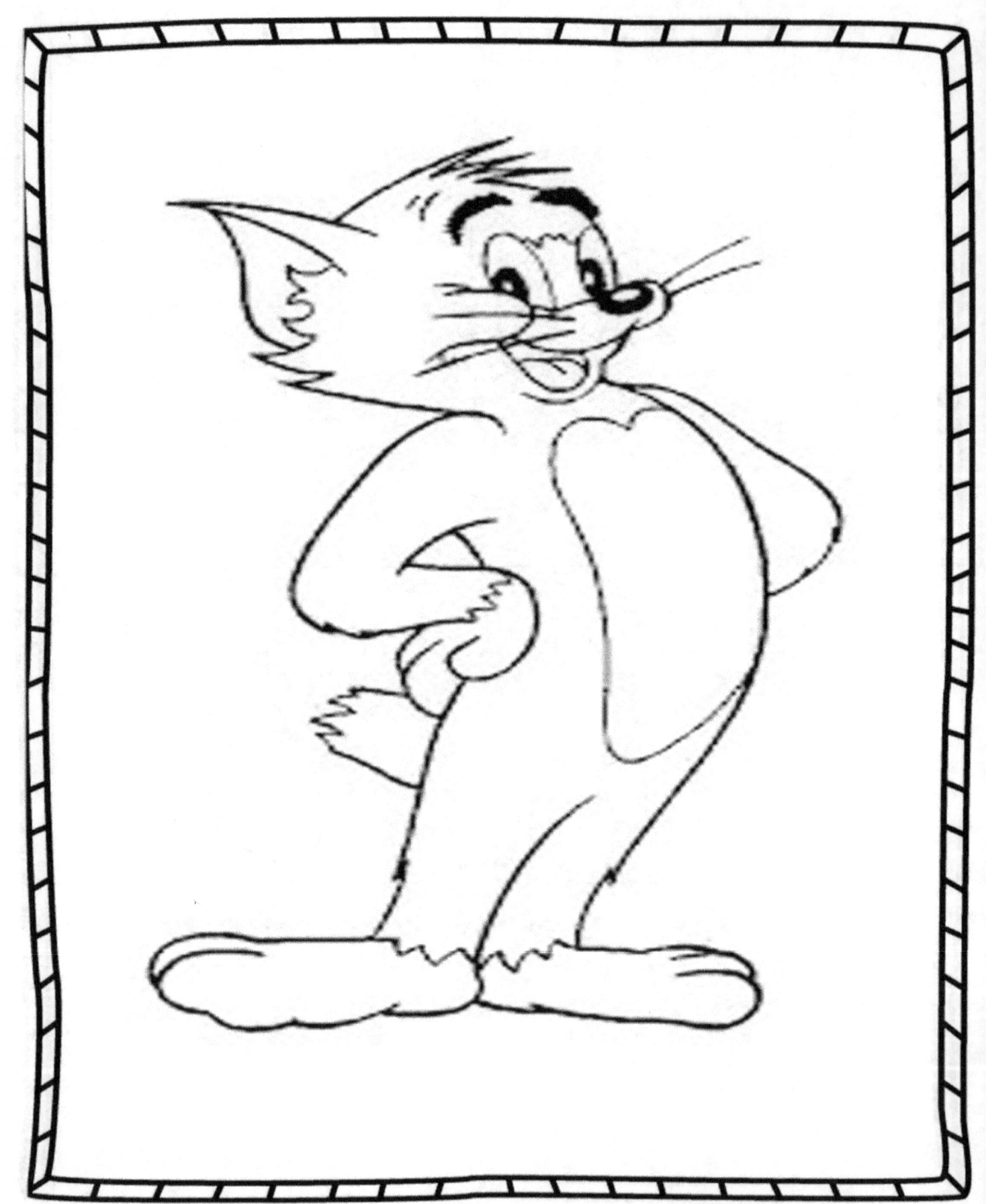

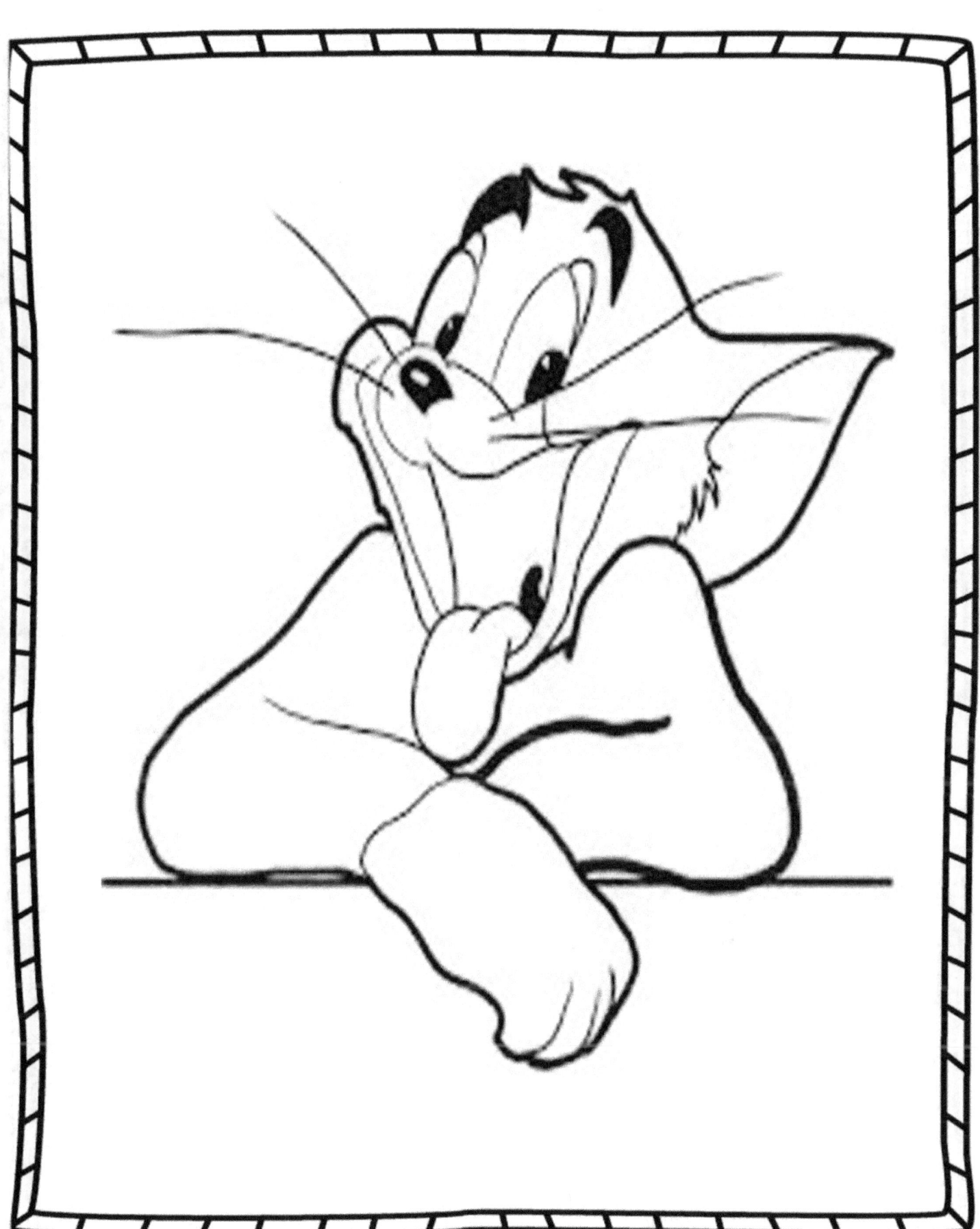

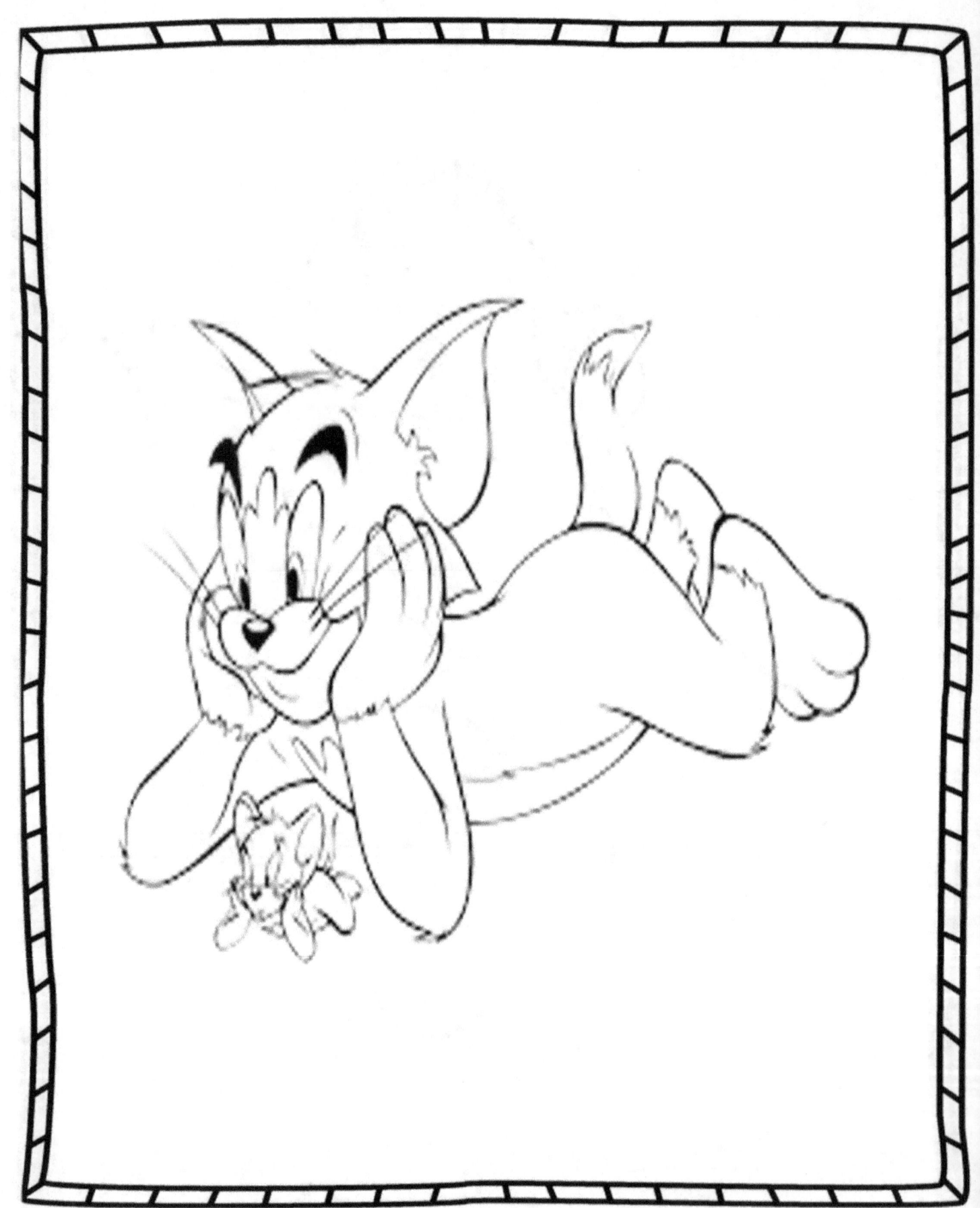

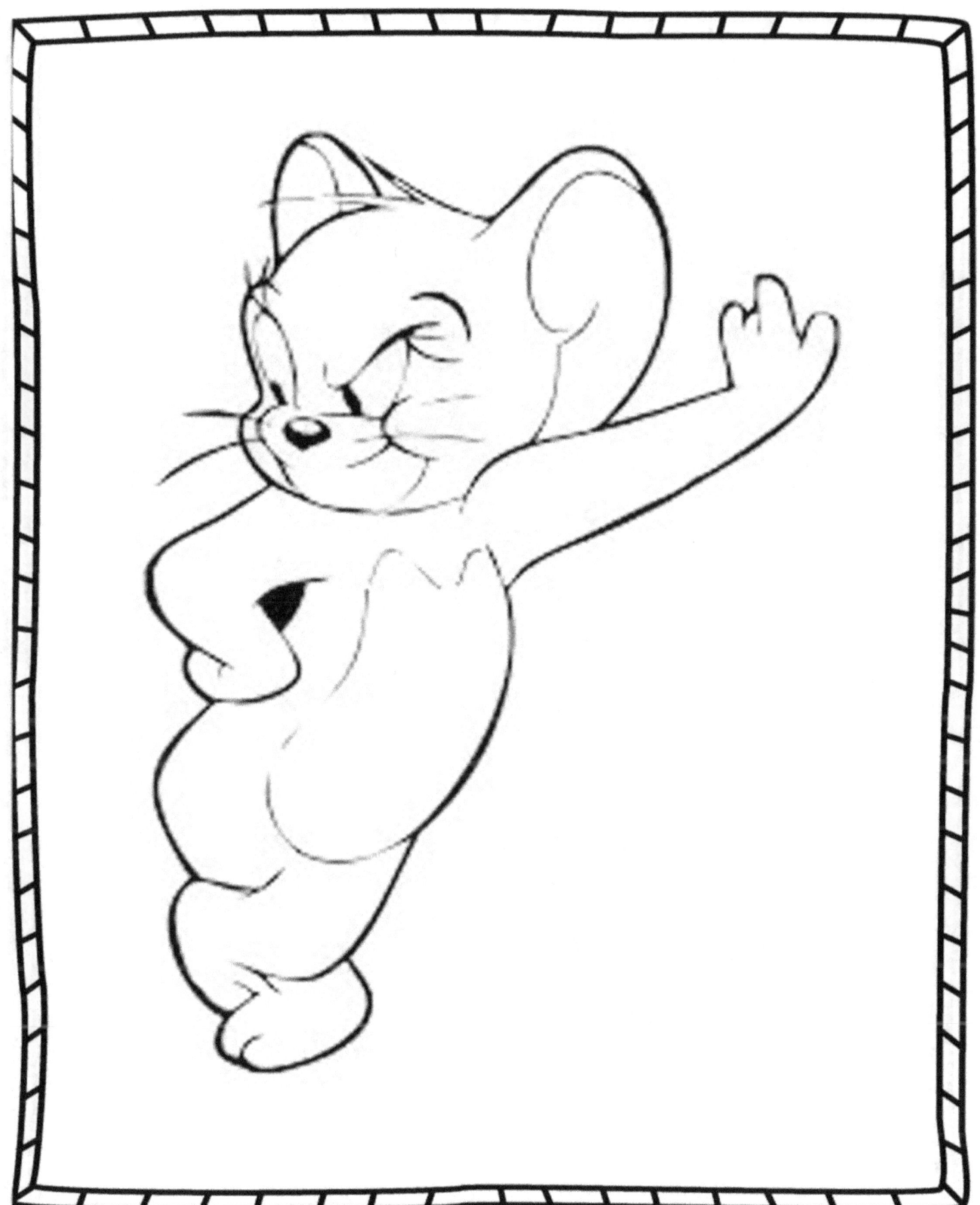

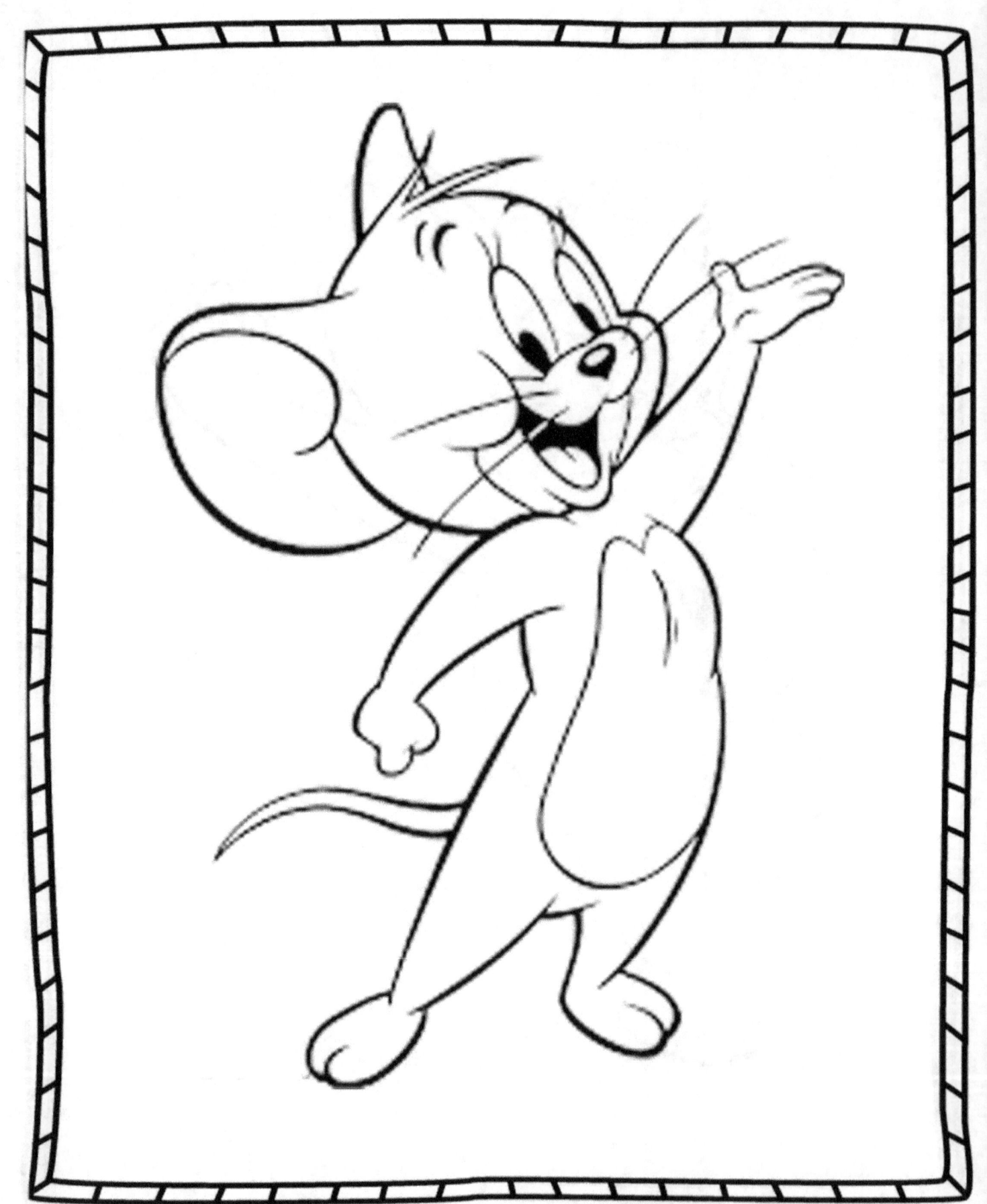

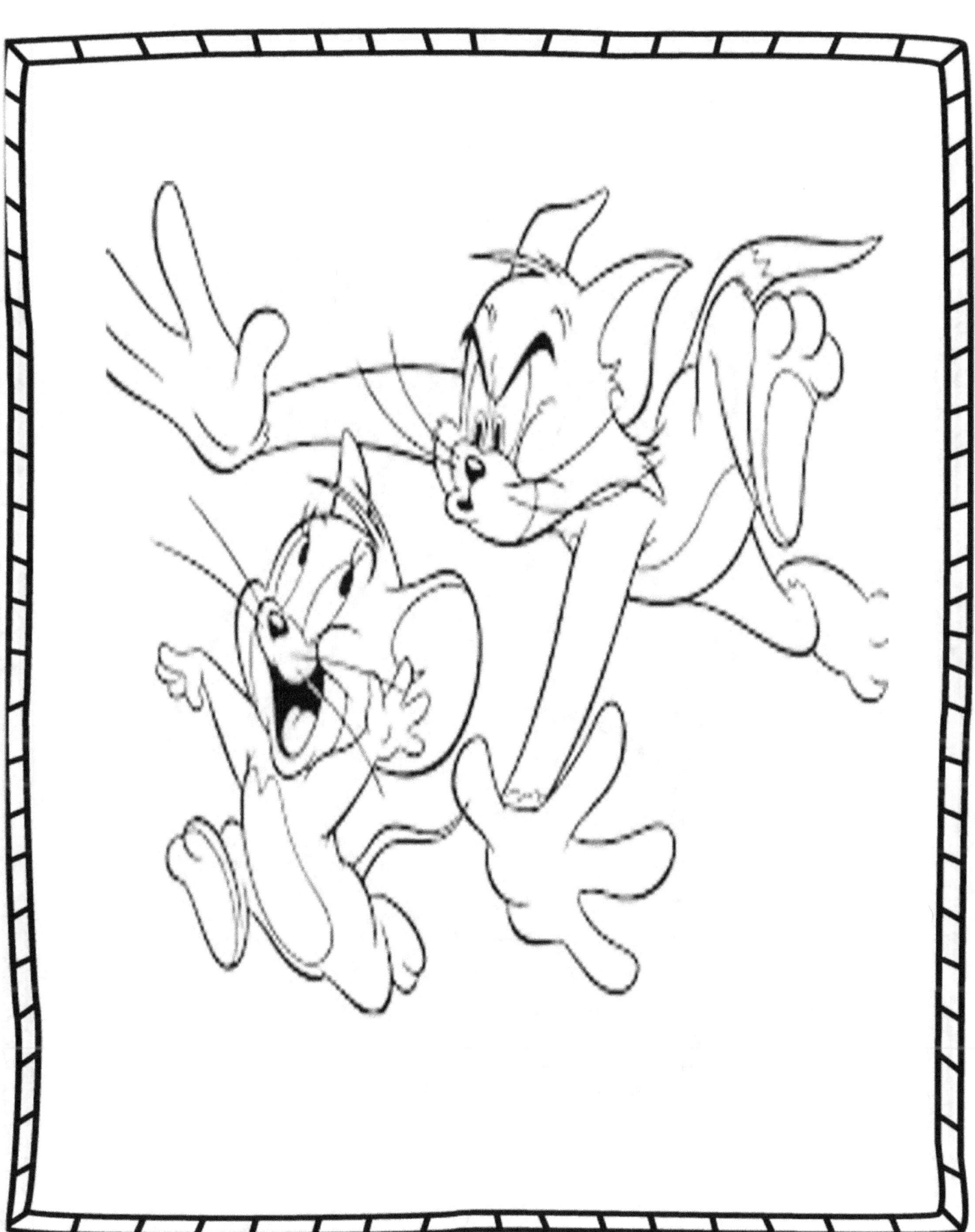

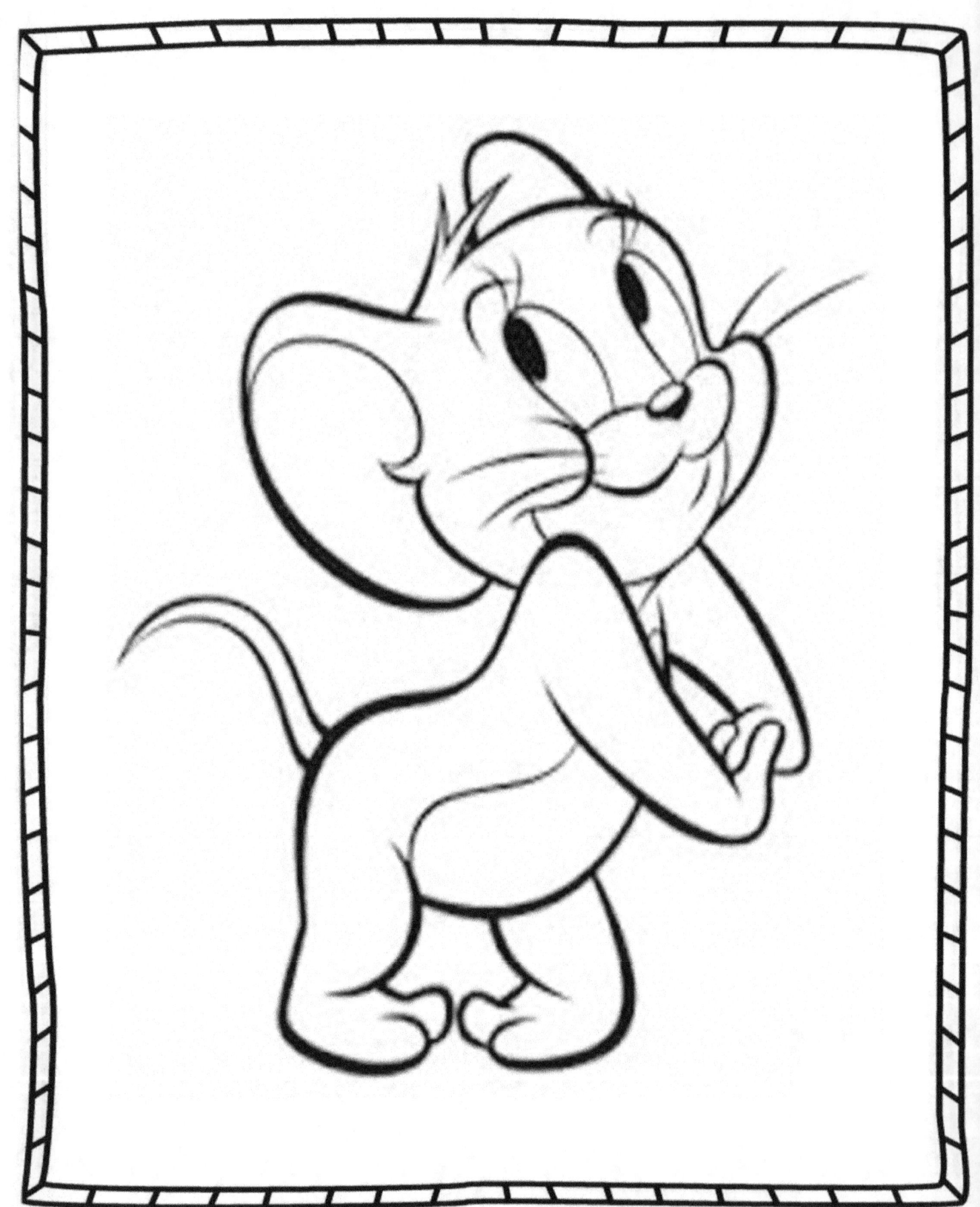

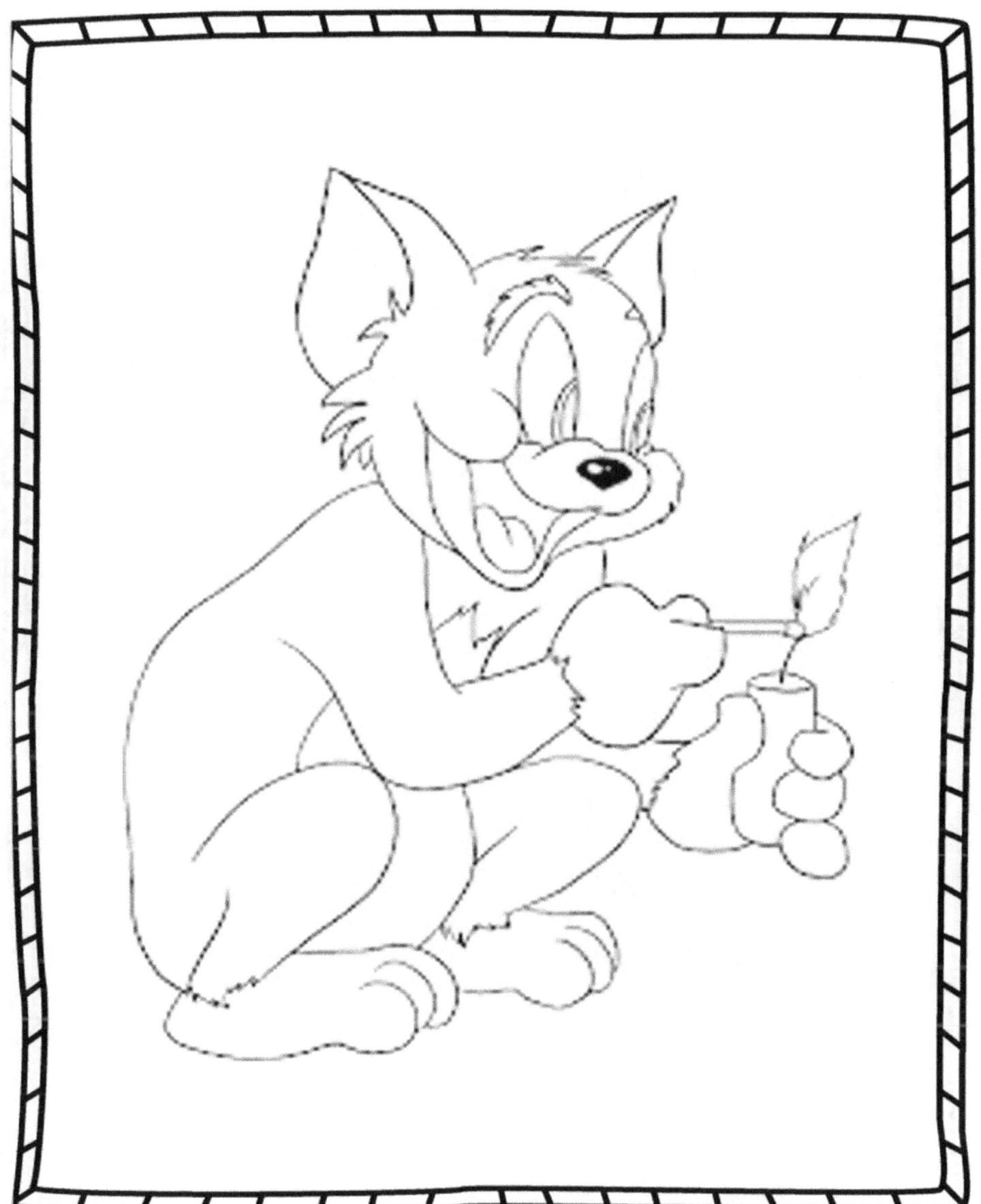

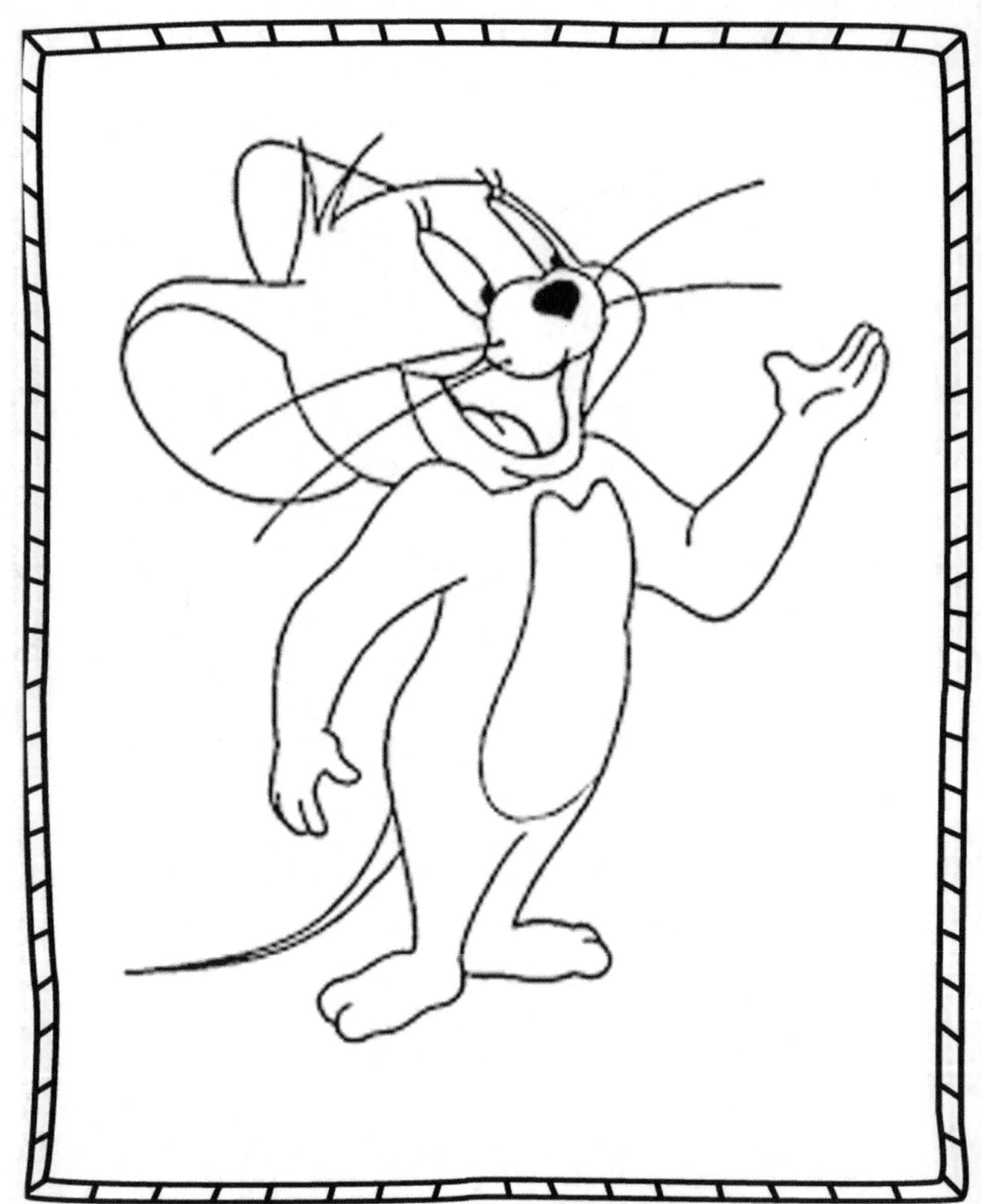

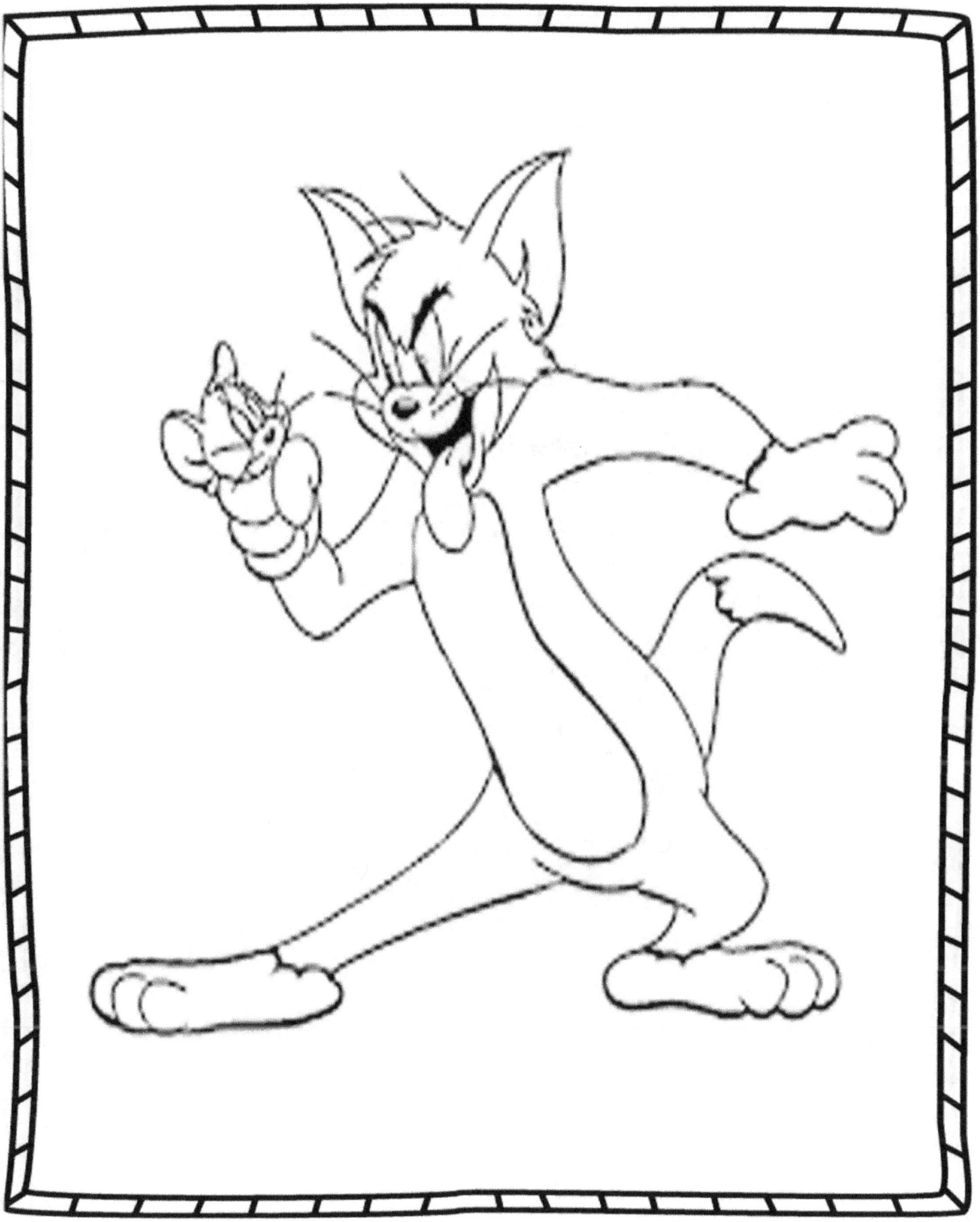

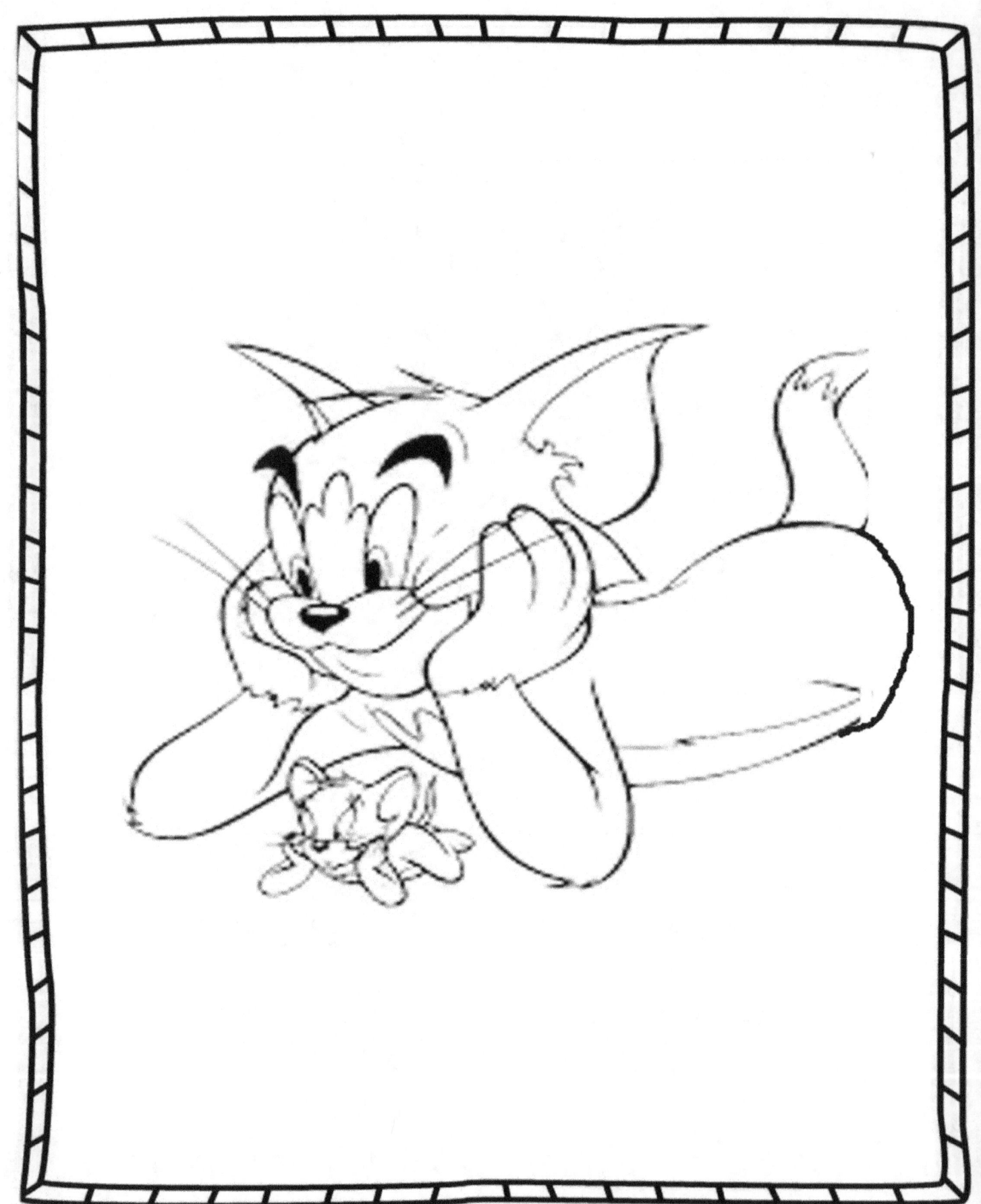

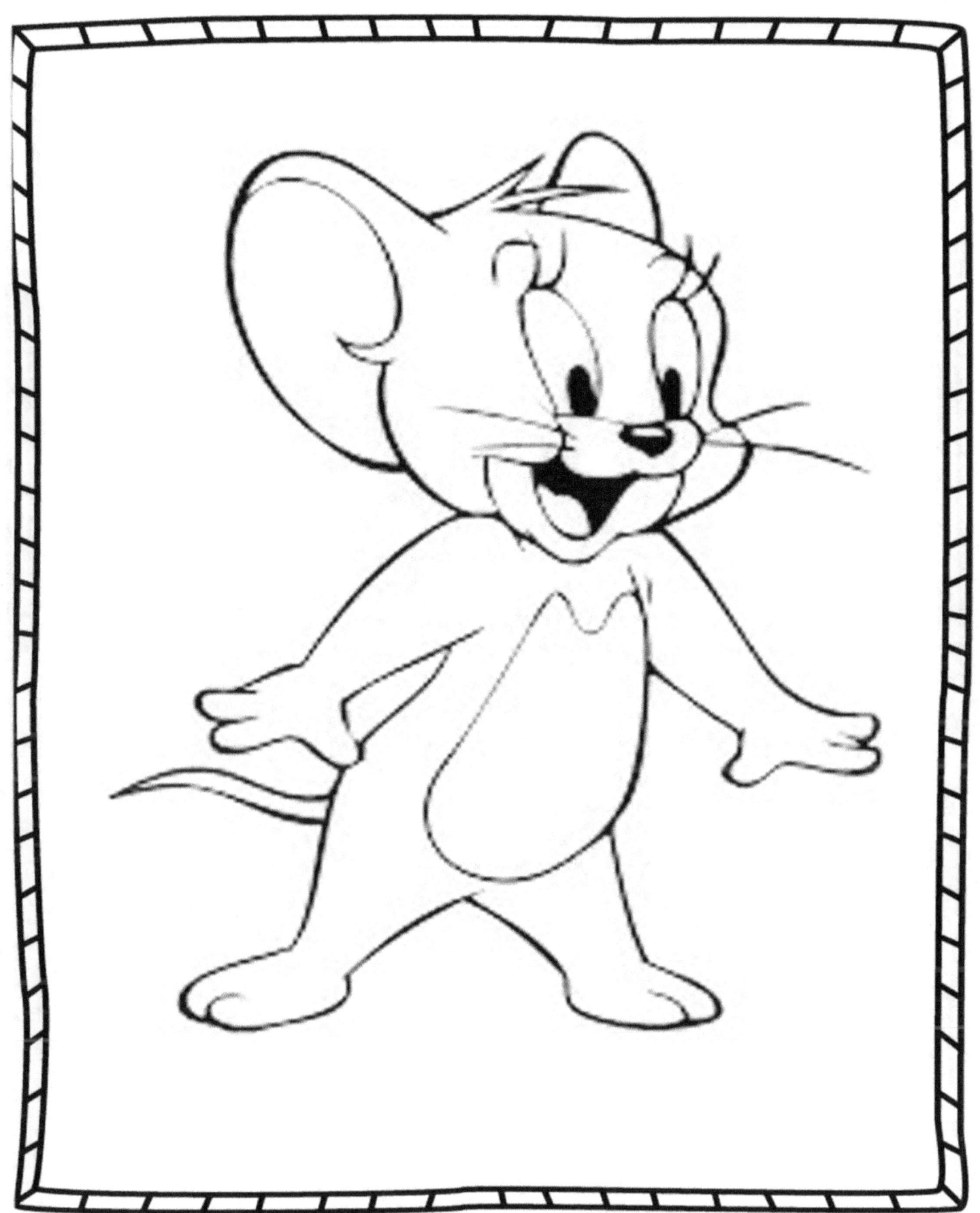

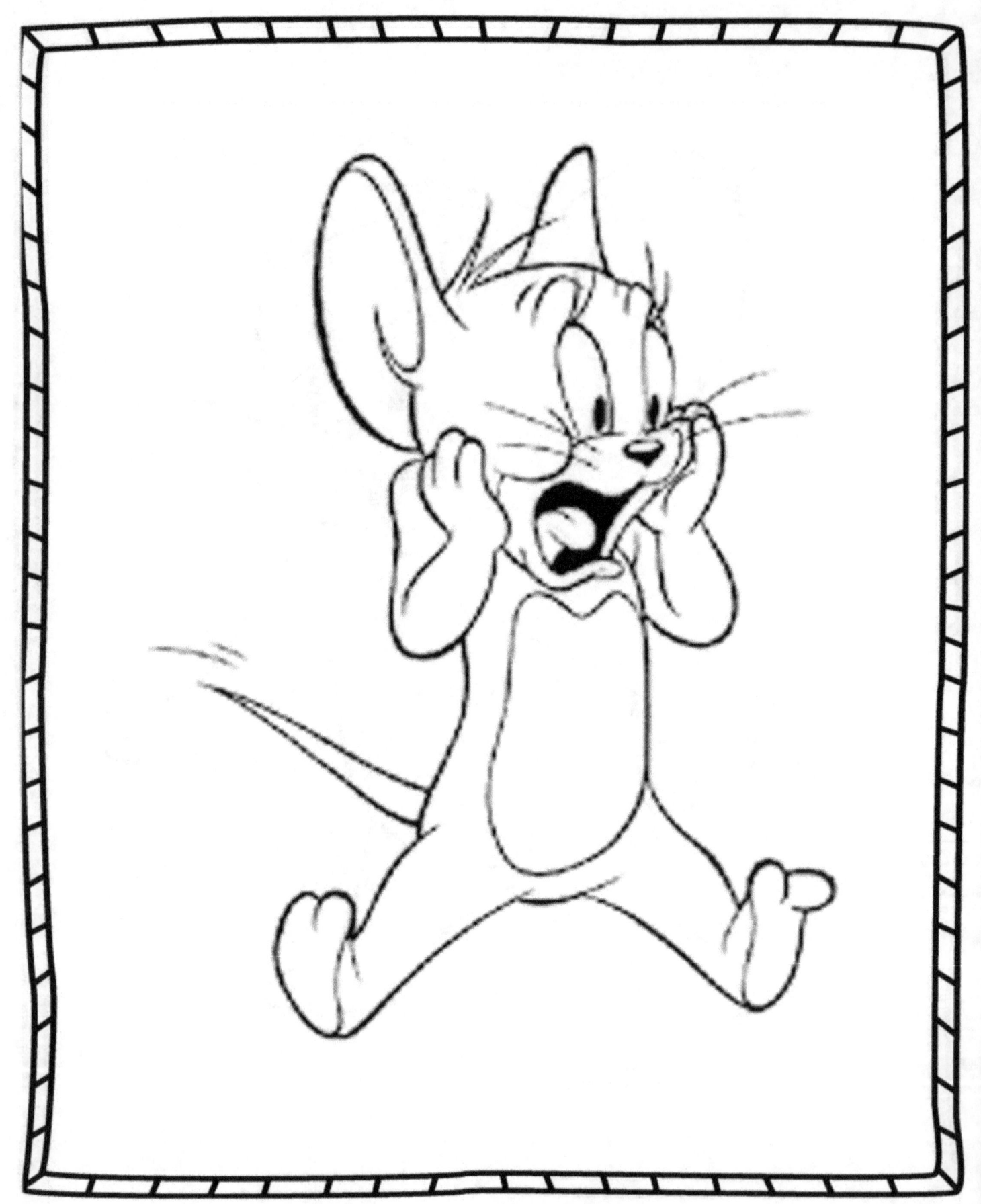

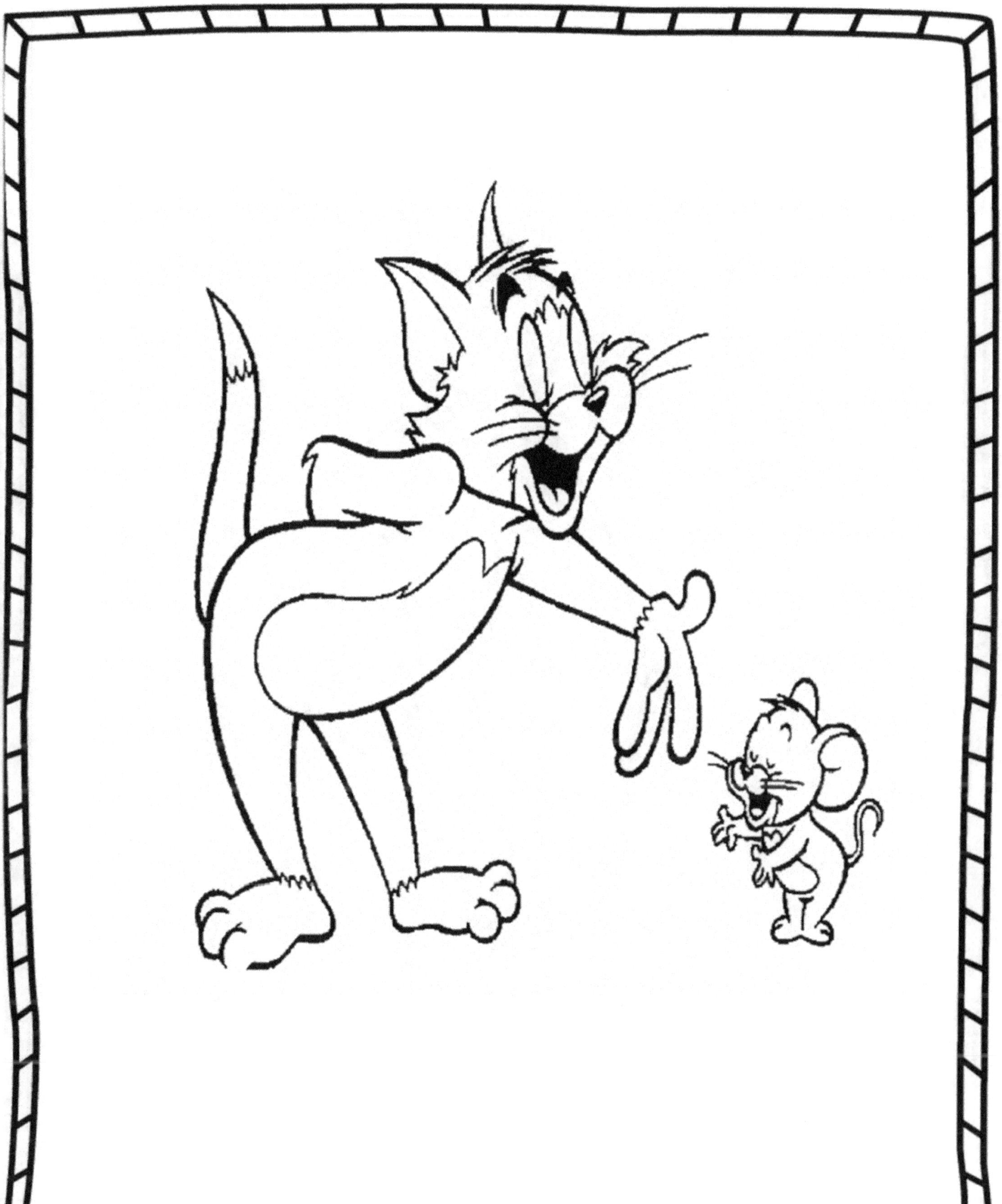

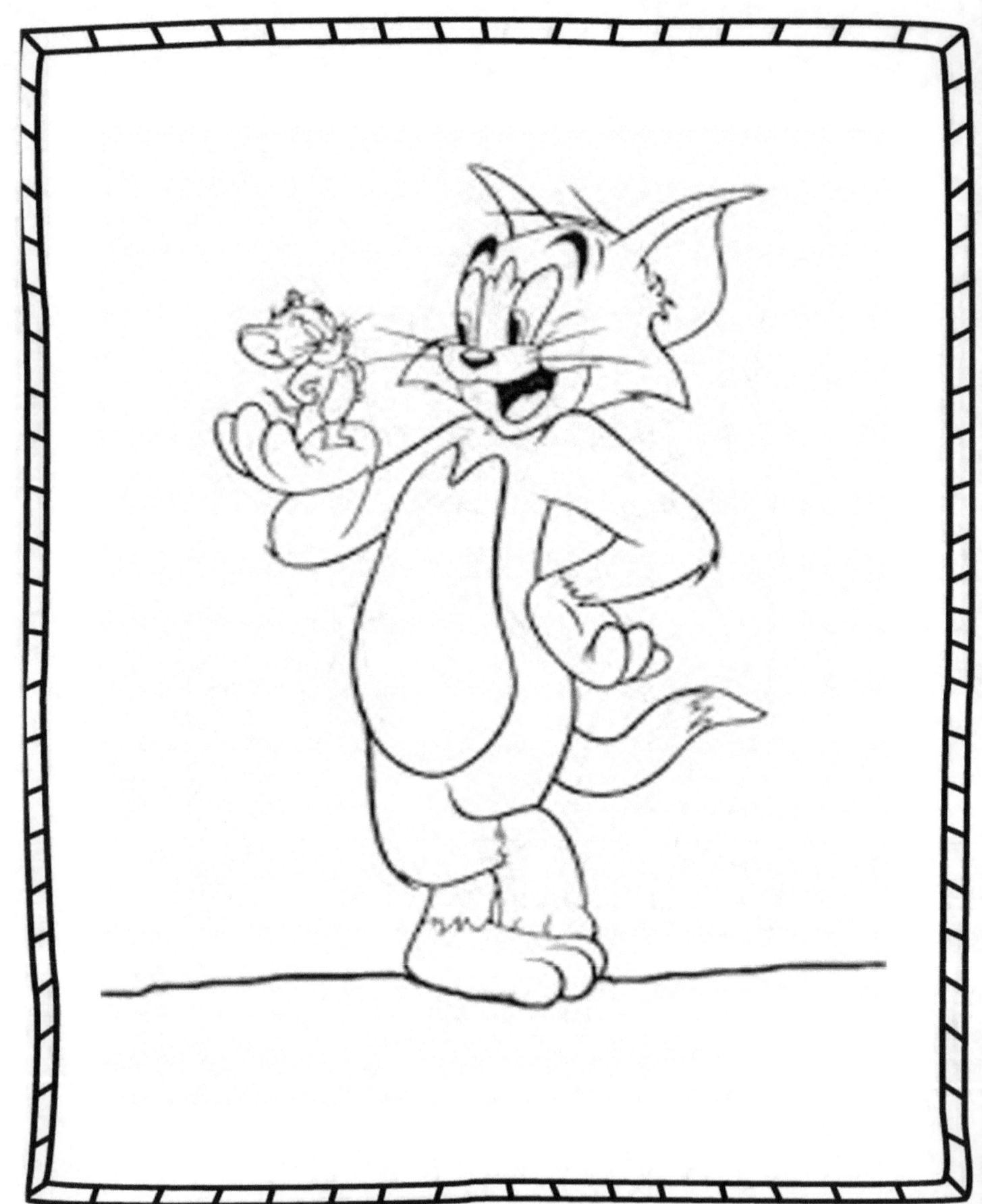

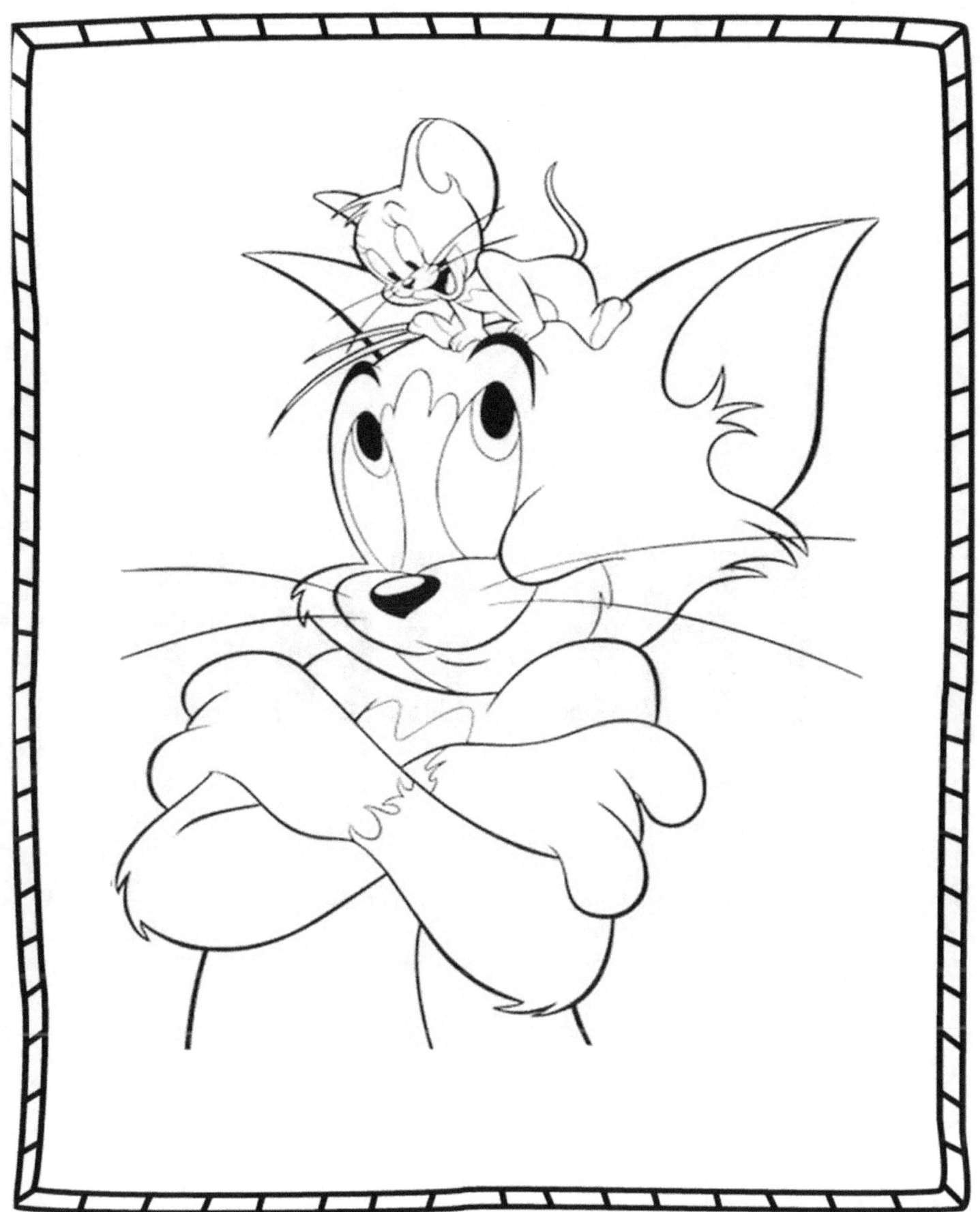

THE END